Bloom Beautiful

{Inspiration for your soul}

Original quotations by Stacey Robbins
Design by Susannah Parrish

www.bloombeautiful.com

GRATITUDES:

For this project:
Susannah Parrish (www.texasusdesign.com) – Pretty sure I don't know how your heart
and your talent fit inside of your body with how Texas-big both of them are.
Thank you for making life, and my words 'Technicolor' and for making me smile every time
I hear the words "road trip" and "red wine."
Tracy Panzarella – You are a force of nature. I stop. I stare. You say, "Let's keep going!"
THANK YOU for being love in action and a new life-long friend.
Carol Meadors – You and that "Yes!" word...both great companions through this project.
Amy Scroggs, Trae Diede, Chris Blue – for help when I needed it most on the details, details, details...thank you!
David Trotter – For being generous with your expertise and experience to make this journey smoother.
Annette Reischl – For your handwritten love all over the pages. Thankful...

For life support:
So grateful for my girly-sister-friends who stand with me and breathe love for me in those every day
and every project kind of ways: Angela Ippolito, Laurie Umbriaco, Joni Brice and Irene Dunlap.
Your presence makes my life profound and full of silly bliss.

For my guys:
Rock, Caleb and Seth – your love encourages me, inspires me and heals me to the deepest part of my soul.
That makes you part of every thought and every word that touches others. Your love is a legacy.
And I am completely, sold-out, wanna-give-you-a-million-kisses, in love with you. Forever.

CREDITS:

Original Quotations by Stacey Robbins
Graphic Design by Susannah Parrish

ISBN: 978-0-615-72937-4

Usually it's the simple things that help us along...

A warm smile
A big hug
A few words

And suddenly we've shifted out of worrying about the size of our bank account,
the laundry pile, or our thighs

And we're reminded of what truly matters...

Simple peace
Deep friendship
The present moment.

And then, we move forward, out of that seemingly stuck place
Into that open space of possibility

Like the seed
Breaking through the soil.

It's life

And it's designed to bloom beautiful

Just
Like
You.

Beautiful you

I would like to go back to the time when I thought I didn't have good legs
but really did.
And the time when I thought I was fat
but really wasn't.
And the time when I thought I was different
and an outcast
but was really a pioneer

and I would like the Divine in me to tell that doubting part of me these words:

"You're doing just fine. You're beautiful just the way you are.
And the people who are going to love and value you are the ones to receive from.
You don't need to keep chasing the ones who reject you. It's okay. Let them rest.

Just know that everything in your life is about returning to the truth of who you are
so that you can live from that place.

Finally.

And again.

...Hang in there honey. You're fine.

You're more 'fine' than you realize.

breathe

These wondering and wandering times that tangle you up sometimes?
They will serve you if you let them remain a mystery
instead of worrying about what you don't know.

Savor the mystery.

Now, just live
and have a good time in between all those deep thoughts
and know that you are perfect right where you are
and just the way you are.

Love is with you.

Always."

question I ask myself

is what I'm doing
flowing from a place of knowing
who I am
or from a place of trying
to prove who I am?

everything changes
when you know
who you are

⊷ you're not the sum total of your weaknesses ⊶

If it feels unnatural for you
to be cherished and treasured
it's because someone/something lied to you.
And you believed it.

Believe something *new.*

"god, help me to make

my thoughts beautiful..."

Be yourself.
Be true to your *heart*.
Live with an unapologetic acceptance of yourself
Create the life ***you*** want.

Not only will you move forward your intention in the world –
you will be sending the message to everyone around you
that they have that same Divinely-inspired freedom too.

you were always so generous that way...

Love who you are

Be true to your VOICE

Speak your truth.

You're allowed to be different.

In fact, we're all counting on it.

 You're what the world's been waiting for.

one of the most beautiful experiences
is being with someone
who's completely
at home
with herself

There's no place like you.

✿

welcome home.

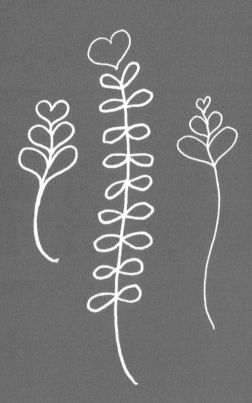

Beautiful us

Let love in.

Notice the flares of excuses and performance – of unworthiness and

"yeah, but's..."

That come into your mind and then,

breathe.

Let yourself sink back into the place where you don't have to explain it,
justify it,
or figure it out

And just let love wash over you.

You don't have to understand it

You can just let it in.

Be someone who can be loved.
That is the healing work of our lives.

One day, in the middle of writing something that stirred up a lot of emotion,
I walked into the kitchen where my husband was standing. I didn't feel brave
anymore and wanted someone to know.

Putting my hands on his chest, I looked into his eyes in that pleading kind of way,
"Why is this so hard?"

He wrapped his arms around me and sighed. Hugging me tightly,
he whispered in my ear,

"Because, it's worth it."

♡ *love* is worth it ♡

when we judge someone
we see the 'mess' in their life;
but when we love someone
we see the 'life' in their mess.

{love someone today}

I must have been feeling brave that night on the couch in his arms,

"Do you love me even though...

I used to be younger
and skinny
but now I'm older and kinda zig-zaggy?

I used to zip around and get a lot of things done
But now, I get the laundry done...
Occasionally?

I used to not have so many cares in the world
But now I get a little overwhelmed and cranky?

Do you love me, even though...?"

He looked in my eyes,
"Honey, I didn't start loving you because you did those things
so, I don't stop loving you when you don't.

He pulled me close and had those little crinkly, smile lines on the side of his eyes.
I knew something good was coming...

"I just love you
because you're *mine.*"

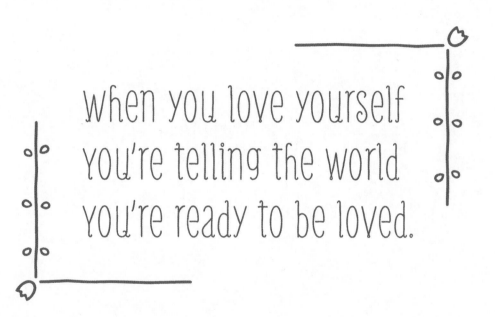

when you love yourself
you're telling the world
you're ready to be loved.

If you're being loved
because you do things 'right'...

that's not love.

When you love people where they are,

they will trust you and want to share themselves with you

when they change.

Love starts now

My husband must really love me;

He never hides the chocolate.

#TRUELOVE

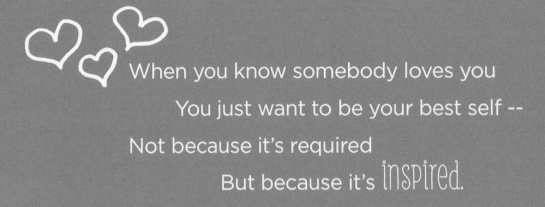

When you know somebody loves you
You just want to be your best self --
Not because it's required
But because it's inspired.

Be inspiring

Beautiful truths

You know how the saying goes, "The truth shall set you free."

So, here's the deal
If you're making assessments of yourself:

"I'm unworthy."
"I'm unlovable."
"I'm undeserving."

And you're not wildly freed by those thoughts

then, it's gotta be
that they're

just
not
true.

Fear won't tell you the truth about Love

❧⸪⸪⸪— —⸪⸪⸪☙

but Love will tell you the truth about Fear.

Seek *Love*

when we live according to our own

heart
and
conscience

we naturally let go of needing people

to like us

or

be like us.

If I'm talking
behind your back

I'm placing those
judgments directly
before me.

Say something *Beautiful*

The minute you feel the slightest twinge of jealousy about another person,
ask yourself this question,

"Am I living out the dreams that I have for my life?"

Because once you do,
and you start taking steps toward what makes your heart sing,

that jealousy will just slip

far

far

far

away.

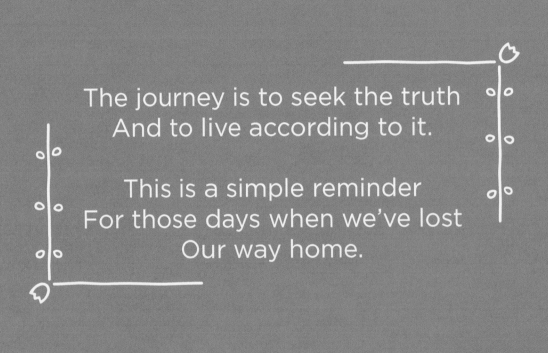

The journey is to seek the truth
And to live according to it.

This is a simple reminder
For those days when we've lost
Our way home.

"I already do have it all."

⇥I said to my self when no one was looking.⇤

Beautiful wisdom

It's all going to serve you:

the frustrations, the seeming setbacks,

the pauses...

they will serve your cause for greatness

and your ultimate 'good'

because all of life is here to support you

if you will see it as your teacher

and your friend.

I remember hearing that a fisherman's net is just a bunch of holes, sewn together.

There are those places in our lives that just feel like one hole after another,
where our dreams are falling through.
Trust me, I get it...

But when we shift our paradigm from seeing these as
"the bad places that need to be fixed,"

to

"the opportune places we get to embrace"
that are calling us to use some creative inspiration

then, we will begin to see those places as friends, not foes –
useful, not wasteful,
beneficial, not detrimental.

With that perspective, we will be sewing those holes together
and making them part of the net
to catch our dreams.

Everything in your life is part of your future dream-catcher.

sometimes you win the prize
sometimes you win the lesson.

DAY OLD OATMEAL IN A BOWL TURNS TO THE EQUIVALENT OF FOOD CEMENT.

{IT reminds me to take care of my messes quickly before they harden.}

When we stay silent
      when we could support

When we criticize
      when we could encourage

When we withhold praise
      when we see something beautiful

We are merely revealing the unworthiness
we feel

    of support
        encouragement
          and praise --

and we are revealing the judgment we have taken on
that there is a limited amount of goodness that can go around

and we feel afraid that we won't get ours
and that somehow, withholding goodness from others
will somehow reserve some for ourselves.

It doesn't work that way.

The moment when you support
when you encourage
when you praise

is the moment you are opening up to the truth
of the unlimited goodness that exists
for everyone
and yes,

that 'everyone'

means *you*.

Choosing to accept ourselves for who we are
and in the face of what we've done
or failed to do
is one of the greatest gifts we can give ourselves
and the people who love us most.

Freedom

Freedom

doesn't come from figuring out how to be loved,

it's figuring out that you already are.

There's a difference when we do things

from a place of

trying to prove who we are

rather than knowing who we are.

One feels forced

the other is a force.

Both may yield results

but one person isn't satisfied until he gets there

the other is satisfied along the way.

Be still

TRYING DOESN'T 'DO' AND 'DOING' DOESN'T 'TRY.'

TRYING BECOMES TRYING.

AND DOING BECOMES RESULTS.

Do something *Beautiful*

Beautiful power

When we're busy working to get power and position -- posturing ourselves
to be close to the inner circle or top of the ladder --
or whatever we have judged as 'success'

we have lost sight that it is our authenticity and integrity
that brings both power and position to us.

It's not about striving, it's about intending.

create authenticity and welcome to your power.
Because being true to yourself brings a power no one can give you
and no one can take away.

create integrity and welcome to your position.
Because being whole with yourself and aligned with your conscience brings a position
of honor that no one can give you and no one can take away.

Once we live in personal authenticity and personal integrity,
every power and every position opens up to us.
Not because we're needy for it
but because we're ready for it.

Live from your heart.

And if someone tries to get you
to ask their permission
before you leap

remember, they don't have the power
to deny you your dreams
unless you let them.

Don't let them.

Be true to you.

The same power of creator-ability to get us into a mess is the same power to get us out.

Sometimes, we forget we're powerful when we're in the middle of stuff.

Love to you today...

In whatever 'middle' you find yourself.

it feels

so very good

to stand up for something that resonates inside of you.

when you don't have to be mean
and you don't have to be angry
and you don't have to be judgmental

but you are just

strong.

This is your life. If you love the script, keep going.

And if you don't, you have the power to re-write it

starting

"The life of my dreams..."

The moment you start being able to laugh at yourself
and forgive yourself
for your imperfections

is the moment you will be healed from the need
to blame others for the parts of your life
you don't like.

And when that happens

your entire life

will shift

away from mentality of victimhood

and toward the mindset of happiness.

Be happy

when you stop seeing people as your problems
or your solutions

you begin to live in the power you have
to co-create with the divine
for your future
your dreams
and your destiny.

the choice is one breath away.

breathe

A friend reminded me today that

choosing to be distracted

instead of present

is a sign of self-neglect.

So, today, the question is before me -- before you -- with every breath:

Are you choosing to be distracted

or are you choosing

you?

seek wisdom
listen to love
follow your heart
no regrets

love someone today
And let it be you

Beautiful you

Bloom beautiful